From Our Home to Yours

Cookies

Ann E. Robson

Title: From Our Home To Yours: Cookies
Author: Ann E. Robson

Publisher: 1449511 Alberta Ltd.
P.O. Box 10181
Airdrie, Alberta, Canada
T4A 0H5

Copyright @ 2019 by Ann Edall-Robson

Cover Photo by Ann Edall-Robson
Interior Photography by Ann Edall-Robson (DAKATAMA™)

All rights reserved. No part of this publication may be reproduced, distributed, or transmitted in any form or by any means, including photocopying, recording, or other electronic or mechanical methods, without the prior written permission of the publisher, except in the case of brief quotations embodied in critical reviews and certain other noncommercial uses permitted by copyright law.

The author and publisher have made every effort to ensure the information in this book is accurate.

ISBN
978-0-9959787-3-7 (Paperback)
978-1-989248-03-4 (E-Book)

Table of Contents

- ~1   Cariboo Cookies
- ~3   Triple Chocolate Cookies
- ~5   Pumpkin Cookies
- ~7   Mom's Cookies a.k.a. Thumb Prints
- ~9   Macaroons
- ~11   No Bake Chocolate Nut Drops
- ~13   Lemonade Cookies
- ~15   Oatmeal Honey Drop Cookies
- ~17   Peanut Butter Cookies
- ~19   Oatmeal Ginger Snaps
- ~21   Helpful Hints
- ~23   Conversion Tables
- ~27   Sneak Preview

Note from the Author

Books by the Author

Caribou Cookies

When I make these cookies, I often think about growing up in the Cariboo. I am reminded of the importance of thinking on your feet, and ultimately, making do with what you had.

2/3 cup	butter or margarine (50 mL)
1 1/4 cups	packed brown sugar (300 mL)
3/4 cup	white sugar (175 mL)
3	eggs-lightly beaten (3)
1 1/2 cups	chunky peanut butter (375 mL)
6 cups	quick cooking rolled oats (1.5 L)
2 teaspoons	baking soda (10 mL)
1 1/2 cups	raisins (375 mL)
1 cup	semi-sweet chocolate chips (250mL)
1/2 cup	M & M's (125 mL)
1/2 cup	toffee bits (125 mL)

Beat white sugar, brown sugar and eggs together until smooth and light in texture. Set aside.

In a large pot, melt butter over a low heat. Slowly add egg mixture to peanut butter mixture, mixing until smooth. Remove from heat and add remaining ingredients. The dough will be sticky.

Drop by heaping teaspoonful approximately 1" in diameter (2.5 cm) onto a greased cookie sheet.

The cookies will spread out to about 3" in diameter (7.6 cm), so space at least 2" apart (5 cm). Bake at 350 F (175 C) for 10 to 12 minutes. Remove cookies from sheets and cool on racks.

This recipe yields 3 to 4 dozen cookies.

Helpful Hint

Freezes well.
Change out raisins for dried cranberries.
Change out raisins for half dried cranberries and half raisins.
Excellent bake sale items for schools and sporting events.

Notes

Triple Chocolate Cookies

1 cup	margarine or butter (250 mL)
1 1/2 cups	white sugar (375 mL)
2	eggs (2)
2 teaspoons	vanilla (10 mL)
2 cups	flour (500 mL)
2/3 cups	cocoa (150 mL)
3/4 teaspoon	baking soda (3.5 mL)
1/2 teaspoon	salt (2.5 mL)
3/4 cup	chocolate chips (175 mL)
3/4 cup	white chocolate chips (175 mL)

Sift together flour, cocoa, baking soda and salt. Set aside.

Cream butter and sugar together, beating until light and fluffy. Add eggs one at a time, mixing until incorporated. Add vanilla. Stir until mixture is creamy and smooth.

Slowly add flour mixture to butter mixture, mix well. Stir in both white and chocolate chips. The dough will be stiff and slightly sticky.

Heat oven to 350 F (175 C). Drop dough by teaspoonful onto a greased or parchment paper lined cookie sheet. Bake for 8 to 10 minutes. Remove cookies from cookie sheet and place onto a wire rack to cool.

This recipe yields 4 to 5 dozen cookies.

Helpful Hints

Freezes well.
Substitute vanilla with Triple Sec liqueur and chocolate chips with orange flavoured chips.
Substitute chocolate and white chips with peanut butter or butterscotch chips or toffee bits.

Notes

Pumpkin Cookies

    1 cup   sugar (250 mL)
    1 cup   mashed fresh cooked or canned pumpkin (250 mL)
    1/2 cup   shortening or butter (125 mL)
    1 tablespoon grated orange peel (15 mL)
    2 cups   all-purpose flour (500 mL)
    1 teaspoons baking powder (5 mL)
    1 teaspoons baking soda (5 mL)
    1 teaspoons cinnamon or pumpkin spice (5 mL)
    1/4 teaspoon salt (1 mL)

Optional – mix, match or not at all
    1/2 cup   raisins (125 mL)
    1/2 cup   chopped nuts (125 mL)
    1/2 cup   chocolate chips (125 mL)
    1/2 cup   dried cranberries (125 mL)

Sift together flour, baking powder, baking soda, cinnamon and salt. Set aside.

Cream sugar and shortening together; add pumpkin and orange peel. Mix until well blended. Stir in flour mixture. Add in your "optional" ingredients if using.

Heat oven to 375 F (190 C). Drop dough by teaspoonful onto greased or parchment paper lined cookie sheet. Bake for 8 to 10 minutes or until light brown around the edges.

Immediately remove from cookie sheet. Dust with icing sugar if desired. This recipe yields 3 to 4 dozen cookies.

Helpful Hints

When preparing pumpkin for future use, freeze in one-cup portions. Before using in your next recipe, thaw completely and drain off any excess juice.
Reserved juice from thawed pumpkin to use in soup broth or added to water when cooking rice. Keep the juice in the refrigerator and use within 48 hours.

Notes

One day while visiting with Mom, I asked her what her favourite cookie recipe she used to bake for us when we were growing up. Her reply went something like this. "You kids liked Haystacks. They were finicky to make when it rained. Shortbread, but you only bake them at Christmas. Peanut butter, not everybody liked those, you know. Thumb Prints. Yes, Thumb Prints were the best." In my hand written cookbook they are known as Mom's Cookies (of course)!

Mom's Cookies a.k.a. Thumb Prints

1/2 cup	butter (125 mL)
1/4 cup	brown sugar lightly packed (60 mL)
1	egg, separated (1)
1 cup	flour (250 mL)
1 cup	fine-flaked coconut (250 mL)
1/2 - 3/4 cup	strawberry jam or preferred flavour (125 - 175 mL)

Cream the butter and sugar together. Beat the egg yolk slightly then add to butter mixture and stir. Add flour and mix well.

Make 1/2" (13 mm) dough balls. Dip into lightly beaten egg white then roll in coconut. Place on a greased cookie sheet. Make an imprint in the dough with your thumb or the back of a measuring spoon. Bake at 300 F (150 C) for 8 minutes.

Remove from the oven and make imprint again. Return to the oven for another 8 to 10 minutes. Remove from cookie sheet and fill the thumb print with jam. Cool.

This recipe yields 2 to 3 dozen thumb prints.

Helpful Hints

Chocolate kisses or toffee bits can be used in place of jam.
Roll cookies in ground nuts instead of coconut.
Freeze cookies without filling the imprint. When you are ready to use them, thaw completely and fill with your choice of filling.

Notes

Macaroons

5 1/3 cups	fine flaked coconut (1.3 L)
1 can - 14 oz.	sweetened condensed milk (300 mL)
1 teaspoon	vanilla (5 mL)
1/3 cup	ground almonds (optional)(75 mL)
1 tablespoon	grated orange rind (15 mL)

Combine all ingredients together. Drop by rounded teaspoon on a cookie sheet covered with parchment paper.

Bake at 350 F (175 C) for 8 to 10 minutes, or until lightly brown around the edges. The middles may appear under baked, but will set up when cooled. Let cool for only a few minutes before removing from cookie sheet. Place on waxed paper and drizzle with melted chocolate.

This recipe yields 4 to 5 dozen macaroons. Store in the fridge or in a cool place.

Helpful Hints

Dehydrated orange peel may be used as well. Reconstitute it with 1 tablespoon (15 mL) of water or orange liqueur.

Notes

No Bake Chocolate Nut Drops

½ cup	margarine or butter (125 mL)
1 can–14 oz	sweetened condensed milk (300 mL)
1/3 cup	cocoa (75 mL)
1 ½ cups	rolled oats (375 mL)
1 cup	finely chopped peanuts (250 mL)
½ cup	peanut butter, smooth (125 mL)

Over medium heat, melt butter. Stir in sweetened condensed milk and bring mixture to a boil. Remove from heat and stir in remaining ingredients.

Drop dough by teaspoonful onto waxed paper lined cookie sheets and refrigerate for approximately 2 hours or until set.

This recipe yields 4 to 5 dozen cookies. Store in the refrigerator in a covered container.

These are very rich in flavour and resemble a truffle in texture.

Helpful Hint

Before refrigerating dough, roll in coconut, sprinkles, cocoa or icing sugar. Let your imagination be the guide!

Notes

Lemonade Cookies

1 cup	butter (250 mL)
1 cup	white sugar (250 mL)
2	eggs (2)
3 cups	flour – sifted (750 mL)
1 teaspoon	baking soda (5 mL)
1–6 oz. can	frozen lemonade concentrate, thawed (170 mL)
1/4 cup	sugar for decorating (60 mL)

Sift together flour and baking soda. Set aside.

Cream together butter and sugar. Beat in eggs one at a time, mixing until fluffy and light in colour. Add flour mixture alternately with half of the lemonade (see hint).

Chill dough for 20 minutes in the freezer or 1 hour in the fridge.

Roll dough into 3/4" balls (19 mm) and place on a greased or parchment-lined cookie sheet. Bake at 350 F (175 C) for 8 to 10 minutes until edges are slightly golden. Remove from oven and let sit for 1 minute before removing from cookie sheet.

Cool cookies on wire rack for 5 minutes. While cookies are still warm, brush them with the remaining lemonade and lightly sprinkle with sugar.

This recipe yields 4 to 5 dozen cookies.

Helpful Hint

If you prefer a stronger lemon flavour in your cookie, add 3/4 of the concentrate to the dough, along with an extra 1/3 cup (80 mL) of flour.

Notes

Some of my favourite recipes are old family treasures that have been passed between generations of mothers, daughters, aunts and grandmothers. Often these recipes come with hand written notes that need to be interpreted, tested and amended. Oatmeal Honey Drop Cookies is one of those recipes.

Oatmeal Honey Drop Cookies

1 cup	honey (250 mL)
1 cup	sour cream (250 mL)
2	eggs (2)
2 cups	oatmeal - quick oats (500 mL)
2 cups	flour (500 mL)
1 teaspoon	baking soda (5 mL)
1/2 teaspoon	each of cinnamon, nutmeg and cloves (2.5 mL)
1/2 teaspoon	salt (2.5 mL)
1 cup	raisins (250 mL)

Cream honey with sour cream until mixed. Add eggs one at a time and stir until incorporated.

In a separate bowl, mix flour, oatmeal, baking soda, salt and spices. Add flour mixture to honey mixture and stir. Add raisins to batter and stir. The dough will be quite loose.

Heat oven to 350 F (175 C). Drop by teaspoonful onto greased or parchment-lined cookie sheets. Bake for 10 to 12 minutes, until dough is no longer shiny.

This recipe yields 4 to 5 dozen cookies.

Helpful Hint

These cookies are quite cakey, not too sweet, and can easily be baked using a mini muffin tin. They are great served with tea.

Notes

Peanut Butter Cookies

½ cup	butter or margarine (125 mL)
½ cup	brown sugar (125 mL)
½ cup	white sugar (125 mL)
1	egg (1)
½ cup	peanut butter smooth or crunchy (125 mL)
½ teaspoon	baking soda (2.5 mL)
1 cup	flour (250 mL)
½ teaspoon	vanilla (2.5 mL)

Sift baking soda and flour together. Set aside. Cream butter with sugars and beat until fluffy. Add vanilla and stir. Mix in egg and peanut butter. Slowly add flour, blending well.

Drop by teaspoonful onto a greased cookie sheet. Press flat with a floured fork.

Heat oven to 350 F (175 C). Bake for 10 to 12 minutes. If you like your cookies chewy bake for 10 minutes or less. Let cookies rest on the cookie sheet for 2 minutes, before moving to wire rack.

This recipe yields 2 to 3 dozen cookies, and freezes well.

Helpful Hints

Split the recipe in half and add in extra goodies for a more sophisticated peanut butter cookie.

Some tasty options include:
¾ cup (175 mL) of chocolate chips, white chips or mini M & M's.
½ cup (125 mL) of finely chopped macadamia nuts, raisins or dried cranberries.
For an extra treat, roll the dough into ¾" (19mm) balls and coat in white sugar before baking.

Notes

Oatmeal Ginger Snaps

3/4 cup	margarine (175 mL)
1 cup	brown sugar - firmly packed (250 mL)
1/2 cup	molasses (125 mL)
2 teaspoons	vinegar (10 mL)
2	eggs (2)
1 1/4 cups	flour (310 mL)
1 tablespoon	ground ginger (15 mL)
1 1/2 teaspoons	baking soda (7.5 mL)
1/2 teaspoon	each of ground cloves, cinnamon (2.5 mL)
2 3/4 cups	quick cook rolled oats (675 mL)
1 1/2 cups	raisins - optional (375 mL)

Mix together flour, ginger, cinnamon, cloves and baking soda. Set aside.

Combine butter, brown sugar, sugar, molasses, vinegar and eggs in a large bowl. Beat on medium speed until well blended. Add flour mixture, mixing well. Blend in oats and raisins.

Drop by rounded teaspoonful onto greased or parchment-lined cookie sheets. These will spread out when baking, so it is important to space them accordingly or you will have one big sheet cookie!

Heat oven to 350 F (175 C). For soft, chewy cookies bake for 9 to 11 minutes. If you prefer crunchy ginger snaps, bake for 11 to 14 minutes. Cool for two minutes before removing from cookie sheet.

This recipe yields 4 to 5 dozen cookies.

Helpful Hint

While cookies are still hot, drape over a 1/2" to 3/4" (13-19 mm) piece of dowelling to create a tube. After they have cooled, fill them with fresh whipped cream or ice cream just before serving.

Notes

Helpful Hints to make your time in the kitchen easier and more fun!

- The recipes in this book have been baked and tested at 3600 feet (1098m) above sea level. Be sure to adjust your baking time to your location.

- Make sure all ingredients are at room temperature. Butter should be soft. Eggs can be placed in warm water (not boiling) for 10 minutes to bring them to room temperature.

- Leavening agents (baking soda and baking powder) should be replaced yearly. To test their freshness, drop 1 teaspoon (5 mL) of baking powder into ½ cup (125 mL) hot water, or 1 teaspoon (5 mL) of baking soda into ¼ cup (60 mL) vinegar. If they don't bubble, your product is stale and needs to be replaced

- Chilling cookie dough (an hour in the fridge, or 20 minutes in the freezer) will give cookies more rise and body.

- To keep cookies soft, store them in an airtight container.

- Make cookies as close to the same size as possible – this ensures they will all be done baking at the same time.

- Fresh ingredients make a difference! Ground spices lose their potency and flavour over time. If you can't remember the last time you bought cinnamon or cloves, it may be time to purchase a fresh container.

- Gently spoon flour into the measuring cup to avoid compacting. Level it off with the straight edge of a butter knife.

- To soften butter, leave it on the counter for a few hours before starting. If you are short on time, frozen butter can be grated into a bowl – it will soften in 10-15 minutes.

- Melon ballers or small ice cream scoops make forming drop cookies quick and easy.

- Cookie sheets should be cool when placing dough on them. To cool a cookie sheet that was already in the oven, run it under cool water for 15-20 seconds.

- Having trouble making soft cookies? Try removing them from the oven a minute or two early. Make sure to let them rest on the baking sheet a few minutes though. They will still look unbaked in the centre (this is the secret!), but will set up as they cool.

- When melting chocolate, it is recommended to use a double boiler instead of a microwave or stovetop. If the chocolate gets too hot while melting it will turn white or have white streaks in it once it is cools.

Our family and its history are an important part of our day to day way of life. Using recipes from several different eras has required us to know the terminology of the time.

Conversion Charts

Oven Temperatures		
"Old School"	*Modern Equivalents*	
Warm oven	300 – 325° F	150 – 160° C
Moderate oven	350 – 375° F	175 – 190° C
Hot oven	400 – 425° F	205 – 220° C
Very hot oven	450 – 500 ° F	230 – 260° C

Spoons	
Conventional	*Standard Metric*
¼ teaspoon	1 mL
½ teaspoon	2.5 mL
1 teaspoon	5 mL
2 teaspoons	10 mL
1 tablespoon	15 mL

Cups	
Conventional	*Standard Metric*
¼ cup	60 mL
1/3 cup	75 mL
½ cup	125 mL
2/3 cup	150 mL
¾ cup	175 mL
1 cup	250 mL
4 ½ cups	1 L

Here is a sneak preview
from the next in our cook book series.

From Our Home To Yours:
Cakes & Squares.

Decadent Iced Chocolate Brownies

<u>Brownies</u>
- 1/2 cup	butter or margarine (125 mL)
- 1/4 cup	cocoa (60 mL)
- 2		eggs (2)
- 1 cup	sugar (250 mL)
- 3/4 cup	flour (175 mL)
- 1/8 teaspoon salt (.5 mL)

Optional Add-Ins (use one of, a mixture, or all)
- 1/4 cup	mini chocolate chips (60 mL)
- 1/4 cup	mini M & M's (60 mL)
- 1/4 cup	chopped nuts (60 mL)

Melt butter and cocoa in a saucepan over medium heat. Stir while melting. Remove from heat and set aside.

Prepare an 8" x 8" pan (20 cm x 20 cm) – lightly oil or grease. Set aside.

In a medium sized bowl, beat eggs until frothy. Add sugar, salt, flour and your chosen add-ins. Pour melted cocoa/butter mixture over dry ingredients and mix well. Pour batter into prepared pan.

Bake at 350F (175C) for about 30 minutes, or until the sides look like they are pulling away from the pan. Remove from the oven and cool completely before sprinkling with icing sugar or ice with a favourite icing.

Chocolate Icing
       1 1/3 cups   icing sugar (325 mL)
       1/3 cup   cocoa (75 mL)
       3 tablespoons butter or margarine
                Softened (45 mL)
       5 teaspoons hot water or coffee (25 mL)

Beat all ingredients together. Add more liquid (teaspoon (mL) at a time) if the icing is too firm. Spread over brownies once they have cooled.

Notes

A Note from the Author

The aroma of freshly baked cookies is powerful! It has the ability to transports us back to the days of our childhood, when life was simple and spirits were carefree. It didn't matter the reason why mom was baking, it was the smell drifting through our home that stirred up a buzz among all of us.

Originally, it was a given that you knew how hot the oven needed to be (wood stove or otherwise), and you knew how long to bake them. Each oven was different and because of this, the length of time to bake might take more or less than the previous generation's rendition of the recipe. We have played with the oven heat (electric) and the baking time until we think we have it right. But remember, where you live (altitude) and type of stove you use might mean you need to tweak these recipes, too.

Over the years, all of the recipes in this book have become someone's favourite. We hope you enjoy our selection of hand-picked recipes, and have fun making new memories with your family and friends. Be sure to record your notes. The next generation will be thankful to have them.

From Our Home To Yours,

Ann Edall-Robson

Books by Ann E. Robson

From Our Home To Yours: Cookies

From Our Home to Yours: Cakes & Squares

Books by Ann Edall-Robson

The Quiet Spirits

Moon Rising: An Eclectic Collection of Words

Birds in my Canadian Backyard

From Our Home To Yours:
Homestead Vegetables - Rhubarb

Purchase Books From

https://www.amazon.com/A.-E.-Robson/e/B00HDE1DBG

AnnEdallRobson.com

From Our Home To Yours-Cookies

www.ingramcontent.com/pod-product-compliance
Lightning Source LLC
Chambersburg PA
CBHW041506010526
44118CB00001B/28